UNDER STANDING JUDGMENTS

A BRIEF GUIDE

Gregory M. Fitzgerald

Understanding Judgments

A Brief Guide

—Disclaimer—

This publication is designed to provide accurate and authoritative information regarding the subject matter contained within. It should be understood that the author and publisher are not engaged in rendering legal, accounting or other financial service through this medium. The author and publisher shall not be liable for your misuse of this material and shall have neither liability nor responsibility to anyone with respect to any loss or damage caused, or alleged to be caused, directly or indirectly by the information contained in this book. The author and/or publisher do not guarantee that anyone following these strategies, suggestions, tips, ideas or techniques will become successful. If legal advice or other expert assistance is required, the services of a competent professional should be sought.

Gregory M. Fitzgerald, Esq.
Managing Partner at Fitzgerald & Campbell, APLC
400 N. Tustin Avenue, Suite 375
Santa Ana, CA 92705
(855) 709-5788
Gfitzgerald@fclawoffice.com
https://debtorprotectors.com

Expert Press
www.ExpertPress.net

Contents

What People Say About Greg:

I can not begin to thank you and the attorneys for everything you have done for me. When this first started in January this was an absolute nightmare since I had just had my first baby and dealing with health issues. You guys took this on with such professionalism and confidence and the outcome was even better than I could have imagined. From the bottom of my heart, thank you, thank you … Thank you.

Know that you made a difference in someone's life. The pressure and anxiety that was lifted each time you reassured me things were being taken care of was priceless. This allowed me to focus my attention on what is most important in my life ... my child and health. I will always think so highly of my experience with Fitzgerald and Campbell
as well as YOU.

Thank you.
TINA L., 4/21/2017

Excellent law firm! I found them on Yelp and decided to give them a call. I am extremely happy I did. They are very professional, responsive and kept me updated every step of the way. Mr. Fitzgerald is a wonderful person, great attorney and he cares for his clients. This law firm went above and beyond for me and I will always remember their cooperation and amazing results they achieved for me. There are many firms out there that do what they do. Please choose wisely. Not all operate the same and after working with Fitzgerald & Campbell, I understand now why Fitzgerald & Campbell are better than the rest. Give them a call, speak to their nice staff and discuss your issues with them. They are happy to listen and happy to serve. A+ for them for being attorney's with a spine. Thank you Mr. Greg Fitzgerald for everything. I am happy to call you my friend and I am grateful for your excellent service and attention in my case. I will refer anyone that is in the situation I was in, to you and your firm. Keep up the great work sir!

THANK YOU!!!
KAMAL C., 3/17/2017

I found Attorney Fitzgerald of Fitzgerald Campbell, APLC after a simple web search and decided to give his office a call for their free consultation. I had lost my father the year prior and was working my way through severe depression so all my bills had suffered during that time and I was truly overwhelmed by trying to figure things out. The reception was courteous and patient during my initial phone call and all subsequent calls for that matter. I quickly received a return call from Attorney Fitzgerald and we began my initial free consultation. Between the fear, anxiety and stress of my situation, Attorney Fitzgerald was great at keeping me calm and truly hearing me out. Even with my financial situation being shaky, he was reassuring that he would do all he could to help me through it and "we" would work it out. He was very clear on what I needed to do from my side so that he could help me in the best way possible. He answered any and all questions without hesitation and even offered answers to questions I didn't realize I had! The communication with the case managers was and remains clear, concise and quick. Any time I needed some information, they were there. Adam Jauregui and Fabiola Parkerson were great about working within my budget to get started on my cases. Even when I fell behind in my retainer fees due to hard times and moving, they worked with me to get everything on track again. Never once did I feel judged, rushed or pushed into any decision regarding my cases. April Inlow and Sam Foster have been great with keeping me informed about the status of my cases and the honest opinions they had regarding what my options were for my next move in any given situation. I have recently settled the first case and April was great in making sure I was able to get the most realistic payment option within my limits. She communicated with me every step of the way. This is simply an excellent office to work with. I would recommend them to anyone.

LISA, 1/18/17

Introduction

Honestly, it's my opinion that most of those holding themselves out as "debt settlement experts" are not experts at all. Many who proclaim to know it best usually have an agenda that is not consistent with the average consumer who is drowning in debt they can't repay. Nor do I think they really care. They certainly can't relate to the physical and emotional changes your body experiences when you are overwhelmed with all the ramifications that come from learning you have a judgment entered against you. In my opinion the best "experts" are the ones who have personally experienced this and survived to tell their story.

That is why you should not care about my advice about debt relief unless I can do more than provide a "title" or letters after my name, or even who I work for, as the basis for my "expertise." Sure, I am confident in my strategies for debt relief without bankruptcy, but I understand you want more than confidence. You want to know that your "expert" (1) really knows what they are talking about and (2) actually cares about your specific situation. So, let me start by explaining why anyone considering debt settlement for themselves should read this book.

I am an attorney and have been so since 1991. But years of school and nearly three decades of lawyering for the "little guy," while certainly useful and important, were not the most important part of my "education" on debt relief generally and debt settlement specifically. My real education on debt started in 2003. I bought an Irish Pub and the next three years were the craziest of my life. Long story short, it turns out I'm a much better lawyer than restaurant owner. Thank goodness! I'd much rather be practicing debt settlement than killing myself by running a Pub every day! I should never have gotten involved in an industry I knew very little about. What is important here is that I was ruined financially.

I owed everyone: food and alcohol vendors, credit cards, insurance companies, even ASCAP (for copyrights for the music played in the pub). I was sued many times over and for just about everything you could imagine. I was sued on my Home Depot card. I was sued by American Express, Wells Fargo, and Bank of America, to name a few. I was even sued in federal court. I found myself with over $300,000 in unsecured debt. If you can work your way out of that hole, without filing bankruptcy, you can claim to have some expertise in debt settlement. Not that I would wish this kind of "hands-on" experience on anyone!

It's not a time I like to think about. It's not a time I'm proud of. But it is a time that forged who I was forever to become. I don't blame the creditors at all. They gave me credit and I could not pay them back. The turning point came when I realized that the problem could no longer be ignored, that I could no longer pretend that denial was an effective way to deal with it. The creditors were not going away, and they were a force to be reckoned with!

The good news was, I was a lawyer. I had legal training. I had counseled clients on debt, knew contract law, and knew bankruptcy laws. I had been doing so for 15 years and I was good at it. I had a successful law practice. Using my lawyer training meant taking the emotional component out of the equation. My approach, like that of my creditor counterparts, needed to be strictly business. Absolutely no one cared how or why I owed the money. They just wanted the money. My analysis had to be completely objective. When representing clients, legal training always required an *objective* analysis over a *subjective* one. This first step was huge as it completely took me out of the denial and self-pity that prevented me from the problem-solving approach I always used successfully for my clients.

When I viewed my debt problems objectively, I had to view myself as a client. The first thing I always did with any new client is get the facts. The true facts. What I refer to as the "ultimate facts": Did I owe? Who did I owe? How much did I owe? How fast was it growing? The simple act of putting on paper exactly who I owed and how much actually empowered me, because I now knew the size of the problem. Before that, I didn't even want to know. This kept me in the dark and afraid of exactly what I was facing. It was the "boogie man." When it was on paper, the numbers may have been bad, but at least I had a picture of the problem. Many times, when we can't identify the problem, we make it bigger than it really is. Quantifying the problem is the first step of every debt relief plan.

Next was the law: What could creditors do to me? What were my options? Was bankruptcy available to me? Was bankruptcy advisable? What rights did I have? You also must be objective about the laws and how judges apply them. Unfortunately, we don't get to apply the laws as we think they should be or would like them to be. I already knew this, of course, but it is a lot easier to tell clients "that's the reality" than to accept it for yourself.

I also knew that the old adage, "The man who represents himself for a client is a fool," was absolutely correct. I did look for an attorney. But all I was told was to "file for bankruptcy." That was not an option for me. I didn't want to jeopardize my home and law practice. Others offered "too good to be true" schemes or "one size fits all" debt negotiators with no real legal training. I was not able to find any reputable attorneys who offered any alternative to bankruptcy. So, I resigned to resolving my own debts myself, knowing that the odds were not in my favor. I was not some brave guy out to show everyone how it's done. I was forced to suck it up to survive. I was not happy about it.

After gathering the facts and applying the appropriate laws, the next thing every good lawyer does is research the opponents and the decision makers. You must know who and what you are dealing with. Who are the players? In this industry there are many: the bank, debt collectors, debt buyers, opposing counsel, the judge. How are they going to come after me? When? What can I really settle for? How does the judge come down on these issues?

There were many questions and even less answers. Most people don't know which questions to ask, let alone the answers. And honestly, unless you do it every day, there is no way for you to know all the answers. I don't know all the answers. But I know a lot of them, and that is why I write: to give you the knowledge I learned, much of it the hard way.

If you are struggling financially and have a judgment against you, and for whatever reason bankruptcy is not for you, this book will help you to learn what you need to know so you can *best utilize limited resources to maximum effect.*

The book you are holding in your hands addresses the aspect of debt settlement known as "judgments." Its content is drawn from my full book on debt settlement, *The Bankruptcy Alternative: Keys to Successful Debt Settlement: A Proven Plan to Work Out Your Debt, Stop Creditors from Calling You, and Move On with Your Life*. It's a bestseller, available on Amazon. That book answers the 10 key questions every person considering debt settlement must ask if they want to complete a successful debt settlement plan:

1. What is a "Debt"?
2. What happens when I default?
3. What are the types of debt and what do the differences mean?
4. What do I need to know about the collection industry?
5. Will I be sued?
6. What are my rights and how do I best apply them?
7. What is the court's role in all this?
8. What is a judgment and what can I do about it?
9. What does a "settlement" really look like?
10. Who is best qualified to create and execute your debt settlement plan?

While *The Bankruptcy Alternative* is more comprehensive, I sincerely hope that you will learn something useful about judgments in this little book. Even an answer to one small question might give you hope that that there is life after a judgment. The first step is often the most difficult. My hope is that by reading this book you will learn that there is some hope for your situation.

This book is not going to guide you on how to settle your judgment. Nor is this book going to "sugarcoat" or oversimplify the process—judgment removal is not an easy road. It will take time, money and perseverance to successfully remove a judgment. It will take a well-thought-out plan based in reality. A plan specific to for your circumstances. A plan based on facts. A plan that incorporates the law as it is actually being applied. Such a plan, in the right hands, can get you debt free. It does work. I know. I did it for myself.

Judgments

A judgment is the court's ruling in a case that determines if a "claim" is valid. It is, in net effect, a court order. Whoever wins the case gets a judgment in their favor. In collection cases, if the creditor wins, it has now been determined that you owe the amount stated in the judgment. If the defendant wins, it has been determined that you don't owe the money. When a judgment is entered against you, it does not mean you must pay it right then. It is just that the matter has been adjudicated as to who owes who and how much.

The judgment creditor can, however, use the judgment to get other "enforcement" orders, such as an order to garnish wages or levy accounts. For these reasons it is easier to understand that a judgment for X dollars is a court order that you owe the amount awarded. Keep in mind that if you are factually "innocent" and never had the debt, it no longer matters. If you have been found to be liable, you can be forced to pay. This also works in the reverse: if you did in truth owe the amount, but the judgment is in your favor, you do not owe it.

You should also know that a judgment is for the amount ordered by the judge *and* daily interest (at 10% annually) *and* fees and costs incurred by the judgment creditor to collect the judgment. It is also enforceable against the community assets of your spouse.

There are three ways that a judgment comes into existence:

1. you agree to it (by stipulation or settlement),
2. the court renders its decision, typically at trial or hearing, or
3. by "default," which is to say you did not contest the case at all (or if you did, the court prevented you from defending yourself as a sanction for poor conduct during the course of the litigation).

When You Participate and Go to Court: Contested Cases

When you participated in the process and there is now a judgment against you, it means that either you agreed to the judgment in writing (typically called a Stipulation for Entry of Judgment) or there was some sort of an ultimate ruling against you. Either the case went to trial or a judge made a ruling pre-trial that the case was over for some reason and it was decided that you do owe the money. Therefore you engaged in the litigation process to some extent (even if it was only to sign a stipulation for judgment). You've responded to the lawsuit in one way or another.

Once the judge enters a judgment, the case is over. But even if you lose, you do have some options on how to proceed.

1. You can appeal the judge's decision. But appeals are very difficult, costly, and time-consuming. They often take a lot more time and money than the amount of the judgment.

2. You can file bankruptcy (if you qualify) and most times you will not be required to pay the judgment. There are exceptions to this such as student loans and taxes, which typically cannot

be discharged in bankruptcy. Also, you can't bankrupt judgments for fraud, elder abuse, intentional injury to another, and other certain types of debt.

3. You can settle with the plaintiff, which means you must give them some amount of money in exchange for a release from the judgment, or what is called a "Satisfaction of Judgment."

1. You can wait for the judgment to expire. That is 10 years after the entry of judgment. California judgments can be renewed, however, and can therefore potentially go on forever.

2. There's one more option that is available. We call it the 747 (as in the jumbo jet) motion. It means that you leave California. A judgment by a California judge is only enforceable in California. It is not enforceable in Texas. Therefore, one way to avoid a judgment is to leave the state. However, you should know there is a mechanism where the creditor can follow you and apply for a "sister state judgment" in the state you moved to. The important thing to know is that a California order, or judgment, is only enforceable in California.

When You Didn't Participate: Default Judgments

Those break down into two categories.

- **Properly Served/Notified (of the lawsuit):** This is where you were served properly and notified about the case, but you chose to ignore it and didn't respond on purpose. (Or at least you did not have a good reason for not responding—"excusable neglect" in lawyer speak.)
- **Improperly Served/Notified:** This is where you didn't know anything about the case or that there was even a case against you. Generally, this is a situation where the defendant was not served correctly. If you don't get the paperwork that you've been sued, you don't know to respond.

In the situation where you were served with the lawsuit, but decided to not respond, you are in the same situation as if you did contest the case (see options above). You cannot come back to the court later and want the case to be re-litigated after you chose to ignore the lawsuit in the first place. You are usually stuck with the result without the option to appeal, though you still have the options of settlement, bankruptcy, wait for it to expire, or the 747 motion.

In the default judgment scenario where you were not aware of the case, you do have the option of making a motion to vacate the judgment. In most default judgment scenarios, the Court did not know that you didn't get the correct paperwork. The court relies entirely upon the proof of service the collection attorney filed in the case. If it is defective (other than as to form), the court does not know that and enters judgment against you, assuming the proof of service is correct. When the service is defective, it's sometimes an honest mistake, sometimes sloppy, and sometimes even fraudulent. Unfortunately, "sewer service," where the server knowingly does not serve it correctly, happens far too often.

I talk to people daily who had no idea there was any case against them and the first they learned of it is when they got levied or garnished. Or maybe they're refinancing their home and escrow asks them, "Hey, did you know there's a judgment against you?" These people honestly never received the paperwork. They have no idea that there was a case against them, let alone a court order to pay money or that they have a lien on their house! It can be quite a shock to learn this.

Three Ways to Get Rid of a Default Judgment

When there is a default judgment against you that you never knew about, there are only three ways to get rid of it. By "get rid of" I am referring to legally resolving it, as opposed to waiting for it to expire or leaving the state.

1. File for Bankruptcy

As mentioned above, there are certain types of judgments one cannot discharge in bankruptcy. But if your debt is the type that can be discharged in bankruptcy, and you qualify for and complete a bankruptcy, then the judgment will not be enforceable against you. This is because a Federal Bankruptcy judge has higher authority that the California state judge who entered the judgment against you. It does not necessarily remove the judgment; it just renders it meaningless. This creditor is not required to file a Satisfaction of Judgment. They just cannot enforce it.

(Note: Judgment *liens* are a different matter. Judgment liens are not automatically removed when successfully completing a simple Chapter 7 bankruptcy. A judgment lien is a different legal instrument than the judgment itself. A judgment lien is a secured instrument and therefore, if you intend to have it removed in bankruptcy, you must get a specific order from the bankruptcy judge. If you don't do this, the judgment lien will remain on your property. Most people who have completed a bankruptcy are shocked to learn this. I'm always shocked their bankruptcy attorney did not tell them this.)

2. Settle the Judgment

This is when you give the judgment creditor money in exchange for a release from the judgment. Sometimes, that settlement will be less expensive than filing a Motion to Vacate or even a bankruptcy. (For more information on settlements, see chapter 10 in my book *The Bankruptcy Alternative*.)

3. File a Motion to Vacate, Seeking to "Set Aside the Judgment"

When a judgment is entered against you and you did not have the opportunity to defend yourself, you have the right to file a Motion to Vacate the judgment. There are three requirements you need to prevail on in order to win the motion:

Requirement 1. You must show improper service and/or "excusable neglect."

For there to be a judgment against you, there must be a "Proof of Service" in the court file. The court would not enter a default judgment without it. This document is prepared by and signed under penalty of perjury by the process server.

You will have to show that this document is defective. Many times, that's not so difficult. It's a factual question. Did they serve you at the address where you lived? Did they have the right address? Were you home at that time? You need to establish that you were not where the process server said you were.

Much of the problem with defective judgments is due to a very bad California process serving law which is the direct cause of many people being caught by surprise by an unknown judgment. California allows for what is commonly referred to as "Substitute Service". As the name implies, the collection attorney can serve a "substitute" and not you. It goes like this:

If a process server goes to your home or work in an effort to serve you personally but is not able to do so (you are not there or do not answer the door), after multiple attempts, the process server can leave the documents with any adult who is present (the "substitute"). The process server must then mail a copy to you at that address, and at that point you have been served! The process server must complete and file with the court an additional form called a Declaration of Due Diligence where they state the dates and times they were at the address and unable to serve you personally. They must also provide a physical description of the substitute person they gave the lawsuit documents to.

The problem with substitute service is that the process server is assuming you live at a certain address because you may have lived (or worked) there at one time. What happens is the process server is going to an old address that you no longer live at. RESULT: you never know about the case. Most people are shocked to learn about substitute service and the complete lack of any requirement that your address be verified. A very bad law to be sure, but the law nonetheless.

You should also know that if you use a P.O. Box for your address, you have made the P.O. Box your "agent for service of process". This means you have authorized them to accept service on your behalf. This makes it very easy on the process server.

Excusable neglect is where you did know about the lawsuit and did get properly served, but have a very good reason for not filing a timely response at the court. The best example of "excusable neglect" is when you hired a lawyer and the lawyer failed to file it timely. Most courts will accept this. Trouble is, inept attorneys usually won't admit to it. Other "excusable neglect" reasons are that you were medically incapacitated and scenarios of that nature. Be advised that it must be a very good reason as most judges will not be sympathetic.

However, it is not enough to merely show you were not served correctly or qualify under excusable neglect. The next two are the usually the biggest killers of Motions to Vacate a judgment:

Requirement 2. Generally speaking, you must make any Motion to Vacate within 6 months of learning of the judgment's existence.

You must show the judge that once you discovered there was a judgment against you, you acted quickly to inform the court of the error via a Motion to Vacate the judgment. In California, that typically is within 6 months. If you don't make the motion within the six-month period of time, most courts will not assist you whatsoever. It will not matter that you were not served correctly. It will not even matter if it was not your debt and they sued the wrong person. What you must remember is when you learn of a judgment against you that you contend is improper, you are on the clock. If you do not dispute it timely, it will remain *your judgment.* I will also tell you that some judges are of the opinion that they don't even have to give you the 6 months!

When it comes to proving when you first learned of the judgment, you will have to convince a judge that you never had actual notice of the lawsuit (proper service or not). For example, if you were not served properly, but found the lawsuit in the gutter two years ago, the court is going to ask why you didn't do anything about it when you found it two years ago. If your response is 'I was not served correctly," most judges will still believe you should have done something. If you can't convince the judge otherwise, you will lose. And trust me, the court does not want to grant your motion, especially in standard collection cases. Why? They believe you owe the money! That, and they already have too many cases to handle and they do not want to add any more.

A lot of people wait for some reason and don't come to us fast enough and there is no longer a way to fight it. This six-month time frame is very critical as courts just do not want to grant motions to vacate judgments, even when they know service was bad.

Requirement 3. Judgments more than 2 years old will not be set aside unless an exception applies.

Finally, subject to a few exceptions, you must file a Motion to Vacate within two years of when the judgment was entered. Many creditors, knowing this two-year rule, will not do anything to enforce the judgment for 2 years. They will intentionally wait for that two-year period of time to pass so that you will be unable to contest it. You can see where these judgments are very nasty, and why I refer to them as "financial cancer" in many circumstances. This is because if you don't owe the money, and you didn't get notice of the lawsuit, you may still have to pay. It seems (and is!) patently unfair, but it happens all the time.

There are some exceptions to the two-year rule in California:

1. If you were on active duty. If the judgment was entered against you while you were on active duty (in Afghanistan, for instance) the court will usually set that aside and give you an opportunity to defend yourself (so long as you meet all the other motion requirements as well).

2. If you were medically incapacitated. If you were medically unable to respond, then the court will usually set it aside.

3. The exception we use most often is that our client has a defense to the case; such as when it is NOT their debt, or they are a victim of identity theft. You must establish that to a skeptical court, which isn't easy. But if you do, the court will set aside a judgment that's more than two years old to give you a chance to defend yourself. The very real problem is that it can be very difficult to "prove a negative". That is, it is hard to prove you do not owe something. If it is your debt, the judgment will stand despite the lack of proper notice to you. In the court's view, which they apply very religiously, there is no need to set aside the judgment when you owe the money. They always say to me: "I agree with you; your client was not properly served. And your client has come in here promptly after finding this out. But this judgment is four years old, and your client doesn't have a defense. Your client admits he owes Discover Card. I am not going to unwind this judgment, even though it wasn't served correctly, because it doesn't matter. He owes the money." So even in these situations, it

can be very difficult to get a Motion to Vacate granted.

4. You can successfully vacate a judgment if you were not subject to the jurisdiction of the state of CA at the time of the service. This typically occurs when you are not a resident of CA and do not have any business or real estate ties to CA.

5. Lastly, in 2014 a new CA Debt Buyer law came into effect where if the judgment is by a debt buyer, you have 6 years (instead of the normal 2 years) to contest the judgment.

I had a case where there was a father and son with the same name, Frank Sr. and Frank Jr. Frank Jr. had access to the mailbox and one day there was a credit card solicitation for Frank Sr. Without dad's approval, Frank Jr. signed it and sent it back. Jr. retrieved the card when it came in the mail and dad never even knew there was a credit card in his name that his son was charging on. When the bills came, who got the mail? Frank Jr. of course, and he kept it from his dad. Dad never became aware of it. Jr. could easily keep the ruse alive for months, even years. Frank Sr. had no idea his son had run up debt on the card in Frank Sr.'s name. I've seen this several times. Another classic example is the receptionist who gets the mail at the small insurance agency. Same story.

This ruse can even go as far as the courts! A lawsuit is filed but wasn't served personally (because of CA's bad "Substitute Service" law). So, when Frank Jr. got the lawsuit, he didn't tell dad. Next thing you know, there is a judgment against Frank Sr.! I've even seen a brother file an answer to a case against his brother to keep the ruse going further! Eventually a judgment was entered against the wrong party. Eventually the judgment creditor did a wage garnishment to Frank Sr., and they levied the business bank accounts! That's when dad found out. The general public tends to think that all judgments are correct and isolated errors can be fixed. It can be shocking to find out otherwise.

Twenty years ago, I think it is fair to say the usual practice by the courts was to liberally grant Motions to Vacate on the long accepted judicial preference that litigants should have their day in court. They should not be deprived of justice or a hearing or due process because of a technicality like defective service. But today is a far different world. The courts are overloaded and crowded. They have more cases than they can handle, and they do not want to re-open any old cases. Especially ones where they believe you owe the money!

You should also understand that even if you successfully get the judgment set aside, **the case is not over**! You now get to defend yourself as though you just got served yesterday. For this reason, if in fact you do owe the money (even when not served correctly), it may be best to settle rather than pay to get the judgment set aside.

A Word about Judgment Renewals, Sister State Judgments, and Other Considerations

Judgment Renewals

Before a judgment is 10 years old, a judgment creditor must file an application for renewal if they want the judgment to be renewed for an additional 10 years. This application is filed with the court. The court enters the renewed judgment, but stays enforcement until the judgment creditor files a proof of service stating that the judgment debtor has been served with the application for renewal. This can be served by mail to the address of record in the case (many times the same wrong address from 10 years ago!). The judgment debtor then has 35 days from the date it was mailed (30 days if it was personally served) to file a Motion to Vacate the renewal.

Because a Motion to Vacate a Renewed Judgment is different that the Motion to Vacate process described above, I strongly encourage all judgment debtors who receive Applications for Renewal of Judgment to file a Motion to Vacate it. Courts are much more receptive to vacating a renewed judgment than a 7, 8, 9 year old judgment. Perhaps the most important fact is that if you win the motion to vacate the renewal **THE CASE IS OVER!** This is unlike a typical Motion to Vacate a judgment that is less than 10 years old! Therefore, the risk of any motion is low, but the benefits are much higher! Do not ignore an Application to Renew, it could be an opportunity for you!

Sister State Judgments

As was stated previously, a CA judgment is only enforceable in CA. Likewise, a Texas judgment is only enforceable in Texas, not California. This means a CA employer can completely disregard a Texas state judge order for a wage garnishment. So, if there is a Texas judgment against you, it has no force or effect and cannot be used to get your assets in CA. This was the basis of my 747 motion mentioned earlier as a way to avoid a CA judgment (fly to another state).

However, due to the "Full Faith and Credit' clause in the US Constitution, the orders of one state are to be honored in another state. What a Texas judgment creditor can do is apply for a sister state judgment in CA. It is an expedited process where they file a certified copy of the Texas judgment asking a CA court to grant a CA judgment which can then be used to seize assets in CA. It must be served, and the judgment debtor does have an opportunity to oppose it, but the reasons are very limited. In truth, the sister state applications are routinely granted, and it is not difficult to get a judgment in another state to become a CA judgment as well. This is one reason the 747 motion has limited appeal. We have fought and won Sister State judgments however, so always consult a lawyer experienced in these types of cases.

What's the Big Lesson on Anything Court Related?

Do not ignore court dates! Do not ignore legal documents! No matter where you find them!

We've talked about those who didn't know about the case and what their remedies are when there's a judgment against them. But what do you do when you have default judgment because you chose to ignore it? That is, you got the documents, but elected not to go to court.

Many people ignore lawsuits for all the wrong reasons. The biggest myth out there has to do with the service rules. People think that if they were not personally served, if it wasn't handed to them directly, or because they "did not sign for it" that they don't have to respond. **Wrong**. As mentioned above, California has bad process serving laws that help collectors. It's so bad, let me repeat: A process server can go to your home or work, *or what he/she thinks is your home or work,* on multiple occasions in an effort to serve you personally but when they are not successful, they can merely hand the document to a third party—the "substitute". They generally provide a description of that individual, e.g., Male, 150 pounds, Caucasian, 50 years old. Then they must mail it to you at that address. Once they've mailed it to you, *you've been served*!

The process server then files documents at the court swearing to all of these "facts". The court takes these documents at face value and determines that you've been served, *even though you never received anything.* Worse, sometimes they go to the right address but give it to someone else who lives there, and that someone does not give it to you. I often hear people say, "I received this document in the mail, but it was never handed to me. I don't have to respond." **WRONG!**

You should *always* assume that you've been served. Do *not* assume that you've not been served. Remember, the court doesn't know if you have the paperwork or not unless you tell them! The court assumes that the documents filed by the process server are accurate—and honestly, so should you. Better safe than sorry. Keep in mind that the debt buyer that has sued you is not really interested in making sure you got notified. They just want to file something in the court that says you were notified. Then they will wait 2 years and ... voila! ... their judgment is now a case you cannot contest!

Another myth on service is people think they must sign something. "I did not sign acknowledging receipt of the documents" is something I hear all the time. That may be true in some other states, but it's not true in California. The process server, even on personal service, does not even have to physically put it in your hand. If he's in your presence and you don't accept it, he can drop it at your feet. Many times, they drop it at the door threshold. Sometimes, somebody is behind the door, maybe looking through the window, so they'll just drop it right there. You've been served. Remember courts are looking for ways to not reopen cases. They tend to believe the process servers because, as one judge told me "the server has no dog in the hunt, Fitzgerald." Therefore, the process server is more believable. You, the judgment debtor, have much more at stake—you do have a dog in the hunt!—and therefore you have more reason to lie about receiving the documents.

Understand that the whole purpose of "process service" is so that the court obtains power over you—and then can order you to do things, such as turn over money. The court obtains jurisdiction over an individual, and therefore has the power to order the individual to do certain things. That is the whole purpose of the "Summons" (you get served with a Summons & Complaint).

A person who says to the judge, "I was never served," or "I wasn't served properly," is literally saying to the judge, "You have no power over me." This, of course, is an uphill battle with the judge—even if it's true. You are attacking the judge's power. Most judges don't like that. I've heard judges say, "You saw the paperwork; you got the paperwork. This is America. If you get legal documents, you come into court. If you don't come into court, you do so at your own peril. Don't complain to me because you got the paperwork incorrectly." That's the way they lean. Their belief is that you have an obligation to respond. You don't get far with the judges when it comes to little technical defects, be it service of process or even the case itself.

Another reason someone might not answer a lawsuit or contest a judgment is because they assume it will be too expensive to hire an attorney. Not true. Most attorneys do not charge for a consultation. Therefore, it costs you nothing to get legal advice There's no cost to you to find out what is involved, and I do so over the phone!

Some consumers assume that they owe the money. Again, litigation is about whether the creditor can prove that you owe the money. You should not assume that the creditor can prove that you owe the money. So, don't assume that you owe it. Nor should you assume judgment balances alleged by judgment creditors are correct.

When you get any legal documents you absolutely must talk to a lawyer and see what your rights or remedies are. You should assume that it's been properly served and answer the lawsuit. Better to be safe than sorry. I think if more people knew about this, they would not ignore going to court, or at least would get some legal advice about options.

What Can Creditors Do After a Judgment?

Real Estate Lien

Creditors can put a lien on any real estate that you own. A lien is like a mortgage on your property: if you sell or refinance your property, they get paid in full out of escrow. They can, under the right circumstances, force the sale of your residence. If you're a California homeowner, and you have a judgment against you, in the right circumstances that residence can be foreclosed upon by a judgment creditor. Very devastating. Additionally, be advised that if you work out a settlement agreement, 99% of the time you are not going to be able to pay that out of escrow. That is, any reduced settlement of a judgment typically must be paid outside of escrow.

Wage Garnishing

Creditors can garnish wages (yours and your spouse's). In California, that could mean up to 25% of your take-home pay. They can also get non-W2 income. Another myth is they cannot get your 1099 or self-employment income. You might think, "I'm paid on a 1099 basis, they can't get my 1099 income." Untrue. A judgment creditor can apply to the judge, to get an order against a third party (whoever it is that pays you the 1099 income) and order them to pay that money to the creditor instead of you. A classic example is real estate agents. They get paid on a commission basis, and sometimes quite handsomely. The judgment creditor can get an order that the agent's broker pay the judgment creditor instead. And that's not limited to 25%. It could be the entire amount that you would be receiving on your commission!

Account Seizing

Creditors can seize your bank accounts and other holdings (you and your spouse's community property) without notifying you. And they can take whatever's in the bank account—or even the safe deposit box—without advance notice to you. Imagine walking up to an ATM or store counter only to find out that the money in your bank account has been levied. They can also seize vehicles and personal items like jewelry.

If a bank account has your social security number on it, the creditor can get it. You might have a joint account with your children for a college fund or something. That money can be seized and kept because your name is on it. A good rule of thumb is that if you have access to the account, if you can pull the money out, so can your judgment creditor.

The other thing that most people are unaware of is that a judgment against one individual is enforceable against that person's spouse. **And it does not matter when you were married—before or after the judgment was entered—or what the judgment is for.** California is a community property state. That means your spouse's current wages belong to you. Therefore, if you have a judgment, and your spouse does not have a judgment against them, your spouse's bank accounts can be seized, real estate liened, and wages garnished. A judgment against you is enforceable against your spouse's community property assets. They cannot get "separate property" in California. For this reason, I've had clients who have divorced so that their wages will then be separate property and not community property.

Judgment Debtor Examination

Judgment Creditors can also do what is called a "judgment debtor examination." (And yes, this can be done to your spouse and other third parties as well.) I refer to this as the ultimate squeeze job. The creditor can ultimately have you arrested if you fail to comply. That's because the court has ordered you to show up in the courthouse, answer questions about your finances, and produce documents. If you fail to do so, you have violated the court's order. That is called "contempt of court" and the judge will issue a warrant for your arrest until you comply. This happens far more than people think.

There was a case in Orange County, California where an individual was in the jail for three years for failure to turn over money that the judge believed he had. Something like $700,000 in cash. The court believed he had it. He said he didn't. The court put him in jail.

Needless to say, a judgment debtor examination is a very powerful tool of the judgment creditor. Do not ignore it. Show up with a lawyer if you can. The creditor can ask you virtually anything. They can get just about anything. Judges are very liberal on allowing judgment creditors to ask for anything. Keep in mind, the judgment is a *court order*. If you don't pay it, some judges see this as not obeying the court and typically are on the side of the judgment creditor.

Judgment creditors use these examinations as a huge threat. They can be very nasty, aggressive, and intimidating. It can also be quite effective in terms of forcing people to come up with money to pay off a judgment.

What Can't Judgment Creditors Do?

The good news is that certain types of income are exempt and can never be seized. Social security, veterans benefits, disability—such benefits cannot be seized by a judgment creditor so long as you contest them. Other types of things that cannot be seized are "tools of the trade". For example, if you are an auto mechanic, your mechanics tools are exempt from attachment. You must however assert your rights and get a court order that the funds or assets are exempt from attachment.

We recently had a case with a client that was in the construction business. They seized his truck. We were able to establish that his truck was a tool of his trade and they had to return the truck. Not deterred, in open court opposing counsel asked, "How much cash does he have on him?" He had $90 in his pocket and they asked for it. We argued against it because that's what he needed to live on. Fortunately, he was able to keep the truck and the cash. But other personal items are at risk, too, like watches and jewelry that they see you wearing. It's important not to go into the courtroom looking like a million bucks. I will also tell you that a judge across the hall would have allowed the truck and the money to go bye-bye.

So what can you do when you're confronted with any or all of these seizure attempts? Every consumer has a right to a judicial review—to ask the judge that the levy, wage garnishment, or other seizure not be enforced. It's called a Claim of Exemption. If you can convince the judge that the seizure is too onerous financially, then the court can say the collector won't get it. If you need the money to pay the rent, if you need the money to pay for medical bills, child care, those types of things, then the court can give you the money back. The court has the power to reduce the garnishment and to modify the amount of the seizure.

Throughout all of this, I would highly recommend that you show up with a lawyer. I refer to judgments as financial cancer. They can be devastating financially. Many times, they're unfair. If you have cancer, you wouldn't operate on yourself or prescribe your own treatments. You'd want a doctor to make an assessment and come up with a practical plan to cure the disease. It's the same with this.

Anytime you become aware of a judgment, you need to talk to an experienced lawyer right away. Don't ignore it and pretend like it's not there. Like cancer, your situation will only get worse unless you act quickly. See what your rights are and what your remedies are. You need someone who understands the system and all your options to protect you and your family.

Conclusion

Knowledge is power. If you have cancer, you learn as much as you can. You find the best doctor you can. You and your doctor will create a plan to fight it. That plan involves treatments that are designed specifically for you.

The same is true with debt relief. Your situation is unique to you: your income, your assets, your creditors, and amounts due are all unique to you. That's why you need to get more information and start to change the way you view your finances. You can continue to make minimum payments, struggling while hoping to get more money—somehow. Or you can start investigating how you can become debt free. Once you're debt-free, you can start to save some money. Only then can you turn around your financial circumstances.

Your first step is to gather information. Talk to knowledgeable people. List your debts. Identify who it is that you owe. Write down the amounts that you owe. Track how delinquent you are. It's difficult to do. You've probably procrastinated because you don't want to look at it. You don't want to even think about it. That's exactly how I felt. But you can change that and say, "Okay. It's time to start thinking about it. I'm tired of stressing about it and not coming up with a practical plan. I don't want to be in the same financial distress five years from now."

If you want to become debt free, I encourage you to look down the road and start creating a plan. It you do, today's pain will be a little more tolerable because you will begin to see that there's hope. You should start the process by looking for a good attorney. When you do, here are some questions that you will want to ask.

- Have you ever tried a case such as mine before?
- Is this type of case your primary practice area?
- Have you had a case against this creditor before?
- Have you had a case against this lawyer/collector/bank before?
- What do you believe would be a successful outcome?
- How long have you been practicing law?
- How long are these types of cases?

- Have you had any disciplinary actions by the state bar?
- Do you do debt settlement, debt defense, collection harassment, and bankruptcy cases? If not, why not?
- Do you do discovery on these cases?
- Does your fee include a trial of the case?

Take it from a guy that has been in your shoes. A guy that made a plan and got out of serious debt. I know how this works and I know the players. We've been doing it such a long time that even some collection lawyers have sought my advice—not only for their own practices, but also for their families. I've had collectors refer clients to our office. We have clients today that work in collection offices. I consider it high praise when your opposing side sends their family to you. That's because they know we are honest, we are reputable, and we know what we are doing.

If you'd like to talk about your situation with someone on our staff, we'd love to hear from you. We are easy to reach, and you can online chat, text, call, or email us without any obligation via our website: www.DebtorProtectors.com. There you'll find information about different types of debts and different types of results. You'll be able to watch a variety of videos on various issues that debtors are confronted with. We even have a newsletter that discusses different issues in the debt world.

The most important thing you can do is set an appointment with our office and talk to us about your situation. Most appointments are *free*. We will help identify your circumstances and will enable you to develop a plan to become debt-free.

Finally, please keep in mind that I know what you're going through. I created a plan for myself, executed the plan and got out of debt. I have a house payment, but other than that, my vehicles are paid off, my credit cards are paid off every month, and everything else is paid off.

I've helped of thousands of others just like you. If you find yourself in a situation where you are needing help, give me a call. I'd be happy to talk with you to answer any questions you may have.

About the Author

Greg Fitzgerald has always been dedicated to protecting individuals and small business from the substantial and unfair overreach of the government and its protected insiders such as banks, insurance companies, and other large crony corporate interests such as debt buyers and collectors. In nearly 27 years of practice, he has represented thousands of clients, tried hundreds of cases, and secured countless victories for his clients.

Greg is married, has two sons, three dogs, and three cats. He lives in Santa Ana, California. For recreation, he enjoys golf, hiking, and family. He considers himself to be a libertarian, a Lutheran, and very fortunate to be able to live and work in California.

Made in the USA
Monee, IL
04 November 2026

67377638R00030